CANTONA on CANTONA

CANTONA
on CANTONA

by **Eric Cantona** and **Alex Fynn**

ANDRE
DEUTSCH

Design **Tim Barnes**
Translation **Raphael Del Burgo** with **Catherine Dey**

Location and studio photography
Copyright ©**1996 Lorenzo Agius/FSP** and **Alistair Berg/FSP**
Styling **Sally Courtis/Ellison Lee**

First published in 1996 by **Manchester United Books**
an imprint of **André Deutsch Ltd**
106 Great Russell Street, London, WC1B 3LJ

CIP data for this title is available from the British Library

ISBN **0233 99045 3**

Printed in Italy by EBS-Verona

A Zone Production

Contents

The authors

ERIC CANTONA has captained both his country and his club. He was one of the main reasons why Manchester United won the Double of the Premiership and FA Cup for the second time in three seasons. As a result he was elected the Footballer of the Year by the Football Writers' Association, the first time a Manchester United player has won the award since George Best in 1968.

ALEX FYNN advises a number of clubs on marketing and television. He also writes and broadcasts on football. His last book, *Dream on: A year in the life of a Premier League club,* was published in October 1996.

Acknowledgements

THIS BOOK was the result of a desire to photograph Eric in a style and setting that would measure up to the man. With a wealth of striking images in the bag following shoots in Marseille and Manchester, it seemed an ideal opportunity for Eric to expound on some of his favourite subjects.

THE IMAGINATION AND SKILL of photographers Lorenzo Agius and Alistair Berg provided the core of the book. James Freedman of Zone masterminded the whole project with cool assurance. Jean-Jacques Bertrand, Eric's lawyer, swept away all obstacles despite or perhaps because of holding the French all-comers' record for use of a mobile phone.

Thanks also to Alex Brunner, who organised the photo-shoots, indefatigable designer Tim Barnes, and Tim Forrester, publisher par excellence. Finally, to say that Raphael del Burgo and Catherine Dey were merely translators is to say that Eric is merely a footballer. They are undoubtedly the Cantonas of their profession.

Introduction

AFTER ERIC RETURNED to Premiership action last October following a lengthy ban due to the Selhurst Park incident, many observers felt he would either be half the player he had been by dint of having to keep his 'red mist' in check, or that he would make a teasing, all-too-brief guest appearance which would be terminated abruptly by some self-destructive gesture. That neither of these things happened is down to a transformation that has been as astonishing as it has been ironical.

Quite simply, Eric has redefined the meaning of sporting excellence. He has been magnificent in displaying the skills of the game and deploying them in the team cause. By resisting provocation (and even on occasion acting the peacemaker), he has also reintroduced a quaint, old-fashioned notion that supposedly has no place in the pecuniary environment of big-time professional sport today: namely, that good sportsmanship is compatible with outstanding performance.

How did this transformation come about? Will it last? What does Eric feel about the past and the future, about people, places and events that are important in his life? It was a privilege to pose the questions and listen to the answers that form the basis of this book.

ALEX FYNN
August 1996

dedicated to **Andres Escobar** (13 March 1967 – 2 July 1994)

Challenge

MOTIVATION IS THE KEY to my success. I'm motivated by a challenge. It's the same in football as in life. What excites me is never to stay still, but constantly to do something new, to do something that interests me. It's not always the same things that give me a buzz, not always the same things that excite me. I need new challenges all the time to fuel my passions. I don't just want things to happen to me; I want to live every moment of my life to the full. I want to feel a buzz.

I want to be like a gambler in a casino who can feel that rush of adrenalin not just when he's on a roll, but all the time. He gambles because he needs that buzz, he wants to experience it every moment of his life. That's the way I want to play; that's the way I want to live my life. I need the excitement of a challenge to make me feel alive.

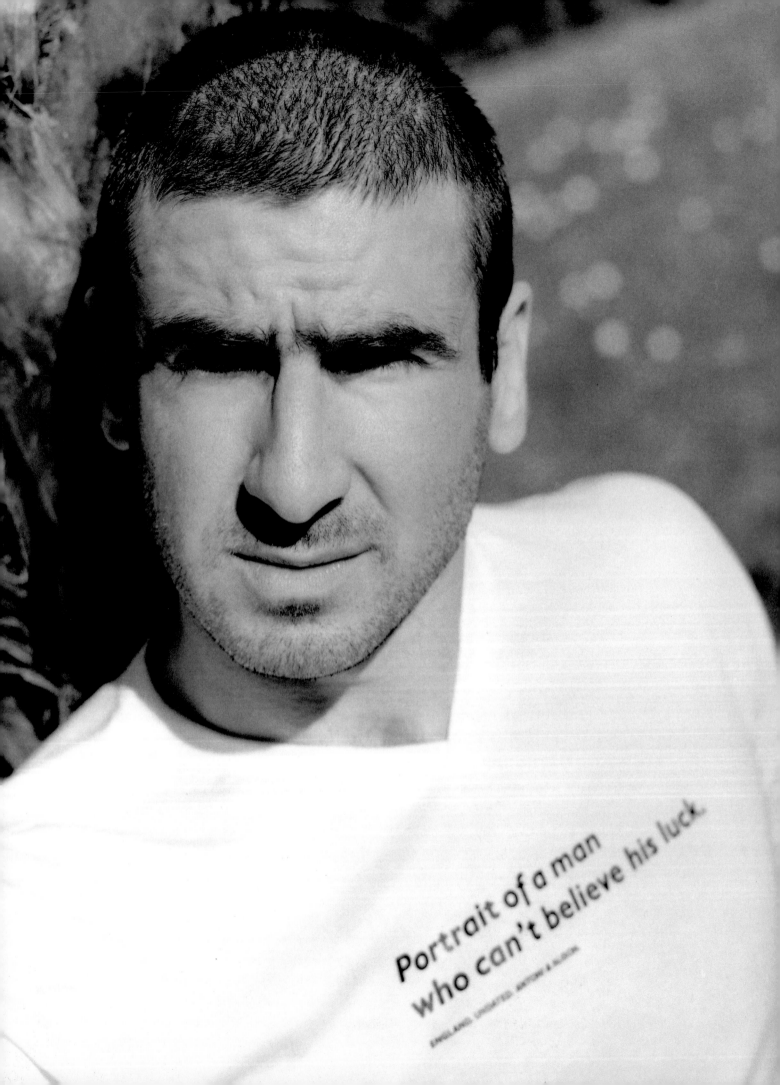

Portrait of a man who can't believe his luck.

ENGLAND, UNITED, WITHIN A WEEK.

Temperament

IT HAPPENS TO US ALL that we get a little sad sometimes, we feel a little melancholy. But being melancholic can be a pleasure too. The human body needs above all to feel alive and sometimes people can't feel the joy of great pleasure. So they find pleasure in sadness. Some people seem to take pleasure from crying. If they can't laugh, at least they can cry, at least they can feel alive in some way. It happens to us all from time to time.

There are people who seem to live their lives entirely by this principle. The Abbé Pierre, for instance, the French humanitarian. People say that he sacrifices himself for others, for the poor, for the needy. But the truth is there's no sacrifice involved. He needs to be the way he is. If he didn't do what he does, he'd die. He does good work, for sure; but we mustn't call all that a sacrifice. He derives great pleasure from it and if he didn't do it, he would either find pleasure in something else or he'd die.

For my part, I strive to be at ease with myself, to find harmony

I often get asked about the change in my temperament since the incident at Crystal Palace. The truth is there hasn't been such a big change. People think I've suddenly learnt to feel at ease with myself, but the fact of the matter is that I was never ill at ease in the first place. Everyone has their bad moments. It's impossible for anyone to say definitively that something like that can never happen to them.

I do, however, have a little more experience now. I've had a lot of time to reflect, and I seem to be able to cope better with situations like that. But who knows? I don't know what I'll be like in the future. None of us can know that for sure.

I'd hesitate to say that what happened was a mistake, or that it was foolish or silly. It was far too complicated to be characterised in such simplistic terms.

There was a time when I would lose my temper regularly, when I felt that I had to stand up and say something about the things that made me angry. I used to take a stand and rage against injustice all the time. Now I know how things will turn out and that has taken the fun out of losing my temper. There was a time when I could derive a

Pleasure

LIFE HAS MANY PLEASURES. There are different sorts of pleasure, from simple joy to total ecstasy. Pleasure can sometimes take you by surprise. In life there are moments when you stumble across a flower, or when you're just outside in the sun, and suddenly the gentlest of breezes caresses your skin and pleasure takes hold of you. Pleasure can be silence after a deafening din. Calm after a crowd. Going high up into the mountains and listening to the silence. But there's another side to pleasure: the excitement of competition. We footballers are a particular breed. We need to hear the roar of the crowd in a football stadium. The more noise there is, the better we feel. But I am aware that there are also times in your life when you need to hear silence, to be surrounded by tranquillity.

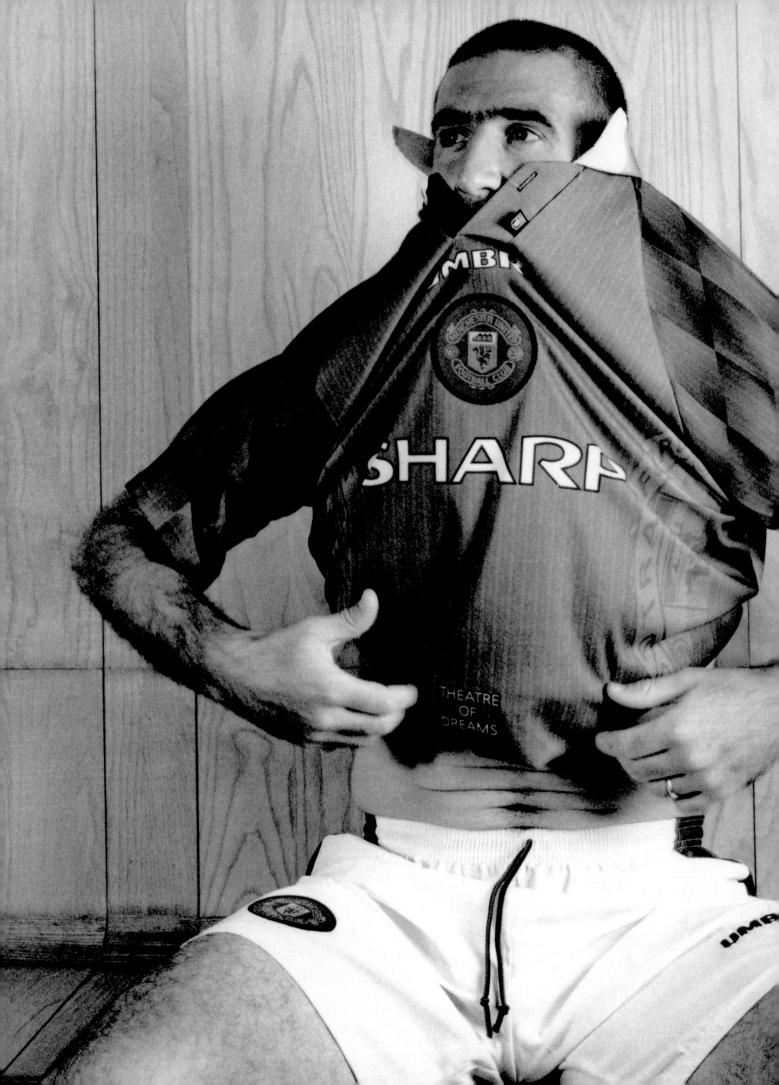

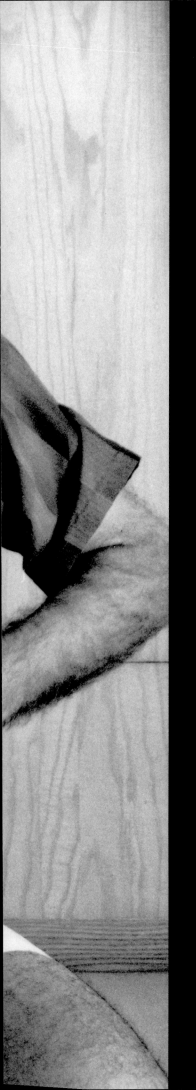

Preparation

THE BIGGEST BUZZ IN THE WORLD is the build-up to a big match. The preparation you undergo; the adrenalin that races through you as you wonder whether you're going to win or lose, whether or not you're going to have your big moment. There's nothing like psyching yourself up for a match that will decide the season: a Cup Final, a crucial Championship game.

Preparation is everything. Focus is the key. The concentration has to be exactly right. It's easy to battle it out on the pitch without having prepared fully and then say "I gave my all". The point is that if you had prepared carefully you would have had more to give and you'd have played better.

When you're building up to a big match, you have to understand the needs of your own mind and body and respond to them accordingly. The match becomes your whole world. Different people have different needs, and the trick is to know yourself so well that you get the preparation right time after time. I know my needs. I know my own body. I need to train hard, to eat well, to drink lots of fluids, and to sleep a minimum of ten hours a day.

Eating the right food is important – as any sportsman will tell you. I don't eat red meat more than once a week. A little red meat helps build my strength, but too much would produce all the harmful toxins I have to avoid to keep myself at the peak of physical fitness. I eat pasta once a day, usually in the evening because you need energy to sustain you through the night. Fast-burning sugars, the sort you find in honey or biscuits, may give you a high for a brief moment, but after a couple of hours there's nothing left to keep you going. That's why just before a match we tend to eat slow-burning foods, like rice, pasta, or potatoes.

Eating well and training hard are fundamental, but that's not the end of the story. Every footballer has to struggle with the problem of balancing the need for hard work with the need we all have to take a

break. I know I need to go out for the evening from time to time, to have a break from football altogether. But I know the dangers, too. For some players, the need for a break becomes an excuse for shirking and they never get down to business. That's happened to me in the past and I now understand how to be careful and avoid it. The trick is to go out and enjoy yourself only when you really need to. If you're just pretending to yourself and shying away from hard graft, you're not being truthful. What's worse, you display a fundamental lack of respect for your colleagues. That's unacceptable. Your colleagues are doing the best they can to improve themselves; it's up to you never to let them down. That's respect. On the whole, it doesn't matter to me what other people do. It's entirely their problem. But if someone's on my team I expect respect from them and I give them respect in return.

You have to give a hundred percent all the time. It's a matter of respecting the fans, too. A matter of honouring all those millions of people who want football to be a game of beauty, a game of passion, a game of glory. In preparation and on the pitch, we give our all. After the match, there will be plenty of time to relax. Before the match, your whole life revolves around ensuring the sweetest and most glorious victory.

Manchester United

Manchester United

COMING TO ENGLAND HAS BEEN A POSITIVE EXPERIENCE. That's due in no small measure to Manchester United. It's the club that's given me the greatest possibility for living, for feeling alive. Because of the sort of person I am, I have a passion for winning. Without the right sort of club, it is impossible to feel that passion. Manchester United has given me the opportunity to share in the sort of glory I have always wanted.

It's not just a matter of the club's long and distinguished tradition: Auxerre, for instance, was a young club which had much less in the way of tradition, but it was a good team. I have to acknowledge that Manchester United's past makes it all that it is today, but I don't concern myself much with the past. It's the here and now that counts. As far as I'm concerned, I belong to this particular part of the club's history, and this is the part that interests me. I want to be part of Manchester United's history, but of a history that stretches out into the future; to ensure that those who come after us can be even better than we are.

The key to Manchester United's success is the way the past is not ignored but is used to build a solid foundation for the years to come. You can see this in Bobby Charlton. He's very much a part of the club's present, part of the club's success today. The club has a living history that makes it the force that it is. All the people who have ever contributed to the building of this club, even players who were active twenty years ago, participate in the club's glorious present in a certain sense. Tradition at Manchester United is not some nostalgic notion consigned to the history books; it is a living presence in the club's dynamic progress.

The cornerstone of the club's success is Alex Ferguson. He has always been the key. Ferguson is the man of the moment, the right man for the job in a club like this. The players burn with ambition, and Ferguson is just as driven as they are. He's a born leader and he has a tremendous sense of energy and drive. He constantly pushes us to win more and more. To my mind, he's the perfect manager for a club like Manchester United and the perfect manager for the players.

Brian Kidd is equally important. He is responsible for training, and it's something he does with such flair and panache that we always enjoy the sessions. That's a crucial part of our success. To enjoy training sessions is the ideal situation. It means you enjoy your work, take pleasure in what you do, and never become bored or feel your concentration waver.

There is a commitment to excellence at Manchester United which make the club unique. There is a realisation that the more we demand of players, the higher our expectations; the more the club has ambitions, the more we'll win and the more the players that come after us will adopt winning ways. It's an attitude that is not confined to the club's philosophy on the pitch.

This is a club where everyone is perfectly suited to their jobs, everyone here is the best at what he does. Not just the best in the vicinity, but the best for miles and miles around, and that's what makes this a truly great club. There is a philosophy of excellence here which makes United what it is today. We aim for the best staff in every position at the club, and they're all fundamental to our success. We not only want the best manager and the best players, we also want the best chief executive, merchandising executive, we want the best receptionist, dietician and so on. And being the best is not enough. They are a team and they have to work well together, to gel. At United, the rest of the staff complement each other as well as the team on the pitch do. And that's the secret of the club's incredible success.

The Fans

PEOPLE ARE SOMETIMES SURPRISED that I give so much of my time to the fans. I'm amazed anyone should find it strange. As far as I'm concerned, it's like belonging to a big family. And if you're part of a family, you have to love each other and have time for each other.

I don't sign autographs out of a sense of obligation. I do it because I know that when fans ask me for an autograph, it's a big deal for them – it might even be a special moment in their lives, a once-in-a-lifetime experience. What you have to remember is that when someone comes to ask for an autograph, it's because they have a passion, and that passion means that if you accept, then that's fine, but if you refuse, it can hurt them a great deal. It will leave an indelible impression on them, a disappointment that will mark them for life. At the same time, if ever they did manage to get an autograph, that too sticks in their memory. When someone asks you for an autograph, it's an important moment.

It's not a case of signing autographs so that people will think I'm a nice guy, but rather that I don't want them to have a bad experience, I don't want to hurt them by letting them down. I don't want to be responsible for leaving anyone with bad memories that can mark them forever. And after all, those same people do a lot for us when they support us, when they sing on the terraces. If I didn't have time for them it would be a sign of selfishness. I'd be saying: "Sing for us, be there for us, support us, let us live those golden moments, but as soon as I come into contact with you and you want something from me I'll turn away from you." I may be many things, but selfish isn't one of them. Of course everyone has some selfish traits in their character, but as far as the fans are concerned, I put them first. It's something people mention about me a great deal, but the fact is that all the players at United feel the same way. We all know what a debt we owe to the fans; we know how important they are.

Interviews

THERE HAVE BEEN TIMES in my life when I haven't given interviews. But I have nothing against interviews in themselves. They can be enlightening for me. If an interviewer asks me a question that I have never asked myself, or that no one has ever asked me, it can be very useful. It can help me to gain greater understanding. Interviews call for a level of self-analysis that can only be a good thing from time to time. Every time someone asks me a question I haven't thought of before, I discover new sides of myself that I didn't know about. There are even times when interviewers ask me questions about something I'd rather not deal with. They can make me confront an uncomfortable truth. And then it's a matter of having the courage to accept it and to come to terms with it.

Silence

FOR A LONG TIME, I refused to speak to the press or the media. So many people had said terrible things about me, some of which I deserved. It wasn't that I didn't want to talk about the Crystal Palace incident, but people wanted me to give an account of myself. As far as I was concerned, the best answer was to win something. Actions speak louder than words.

Teamwork

Teamwork

I FIND IT IMPOSSIBLE to comment on my own abilities. Football is a team game, and one can only ever talk about oneself in the context of the team. On the whole, I find it difficult to discuss the merits of other players too. I prefer to talk about teams and the team game. Victory is for the whole team. That's what counts in every match. We strikers have a job to do: scoring goals. Defenders have a different job: to stop opposing strikers. But we are all on the same side and we are all working towards victory for the team; defenders to defend, strikers to finish. It's a team effort.

The only time when individual effort is uppermost is when a penalty is being taken. Only then is there the sense that the player is out there on his own. Penalties give you the briefest of moments to achieve the ultimate buzz. When the whistle blows, you have only a few seconds to perform.

But they also bring with them a huge weight of responsibility. When you score a penalty, there's a sense that you've done only what was expected of you; yet as you stand there, there's always that niggling doubt in the back of your mind, the possibility that you might not score. A player who scores a penalty is forgotten; the penalty-takers that people remember are the people who have missed, like Gareth Southgate. Out there in the middle on your own, there remains that small but persistent element of risk. You know it should be straightforward to score, though in reality it's not at all easy – and that's what gives you a buzz. The risk involved means the penalty represents an ephemeral but exciting challenge.

Ultimately, victory is seldom about an individual effort. It's about everyone pulling together to succeed. It's about the whole team working side by side to score goals. If you lose, it can be one of two things: either you haven't pulled together as a team and haven't given your all; or you did your best, but the other side was better.

The secret of football, and of team performance, is harmony. True harmony is equivalent to perfection, to beauty. Think of the movement of a champion gymnast, or the perfect synchrony of a whole symphony orchestra playing together. Harmony can be everywhere: in music, in the mind and the body, in a football team's will to succeed; and it's this perfect understanding, this combining of forces that makes winning possible. Harmony in a team means everybody playing together and thinking as one. In the end it's all about getting the ball in the back of the net, about having that perfect touch when you have possession. This can only come from the combined efforts of all the players.

It comes down to instinctive communication and understanding. There must be a kind of unity of purpose in a team. The mind of every player must be focused on the same strategy. The more in tune the members of a team are, the greater its strength is and the better their game is to watch. There should always be a balance between attack and defence. That's the key to success.

Seven

I DON'T REALLY HAVE SUPERSTITIONS, but when you're successful, people start pointing out habits you have and it becomes very hard to ditch them in case you break the spell.

Certain small details have come to be important to me. Like the number 7. I've been playing in a number 7 shirt for the last few seasons. I never asked for that number: it started completely by chance. It just happened because when I first joined Manchester United, Robson was injured and his number was 7. At that time, people didn't always have to have their own number as they do today. So I took his number and carried on playing with it. As it turned out, the number became very significant for me: my daughter was born on the 7 June, for instance. I've got used to being a number 7 and I'd like to continue that way because it's certainly been very successful for me. It's become a habit, maybe even a superstition.

I don't want to change a winning formula. It's the only area of my life in which I'd rather not take risks, because my desire to win is too great. Winning is too important to take risks. Every minute detail that can make a victory possible has to be attended to. That's the difference between winning and losing

England

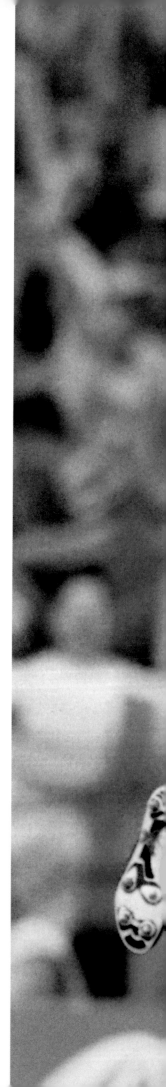

BEFORE EURO '96, many people questioned the abilities of the England team at international level. England deserved their success in the tournament. They had the discipline, they had the imagination and they played attractive football. So many other teams in the competition played a boring, unimaginative game with too many defenders and too many players in midfield. England played exciting football. Technically they were impressive and the passing on the wings was excellent. England were just very unlucky not to win.

Despite what the critics say, the England team proved what attractive football they can play. I wanted England to prove those critics wrong and to go all the way in the competition. That's why I supported England. Everyone was talking about them: they're the kind of side that can inspire you. I was very sad when they lost.

English football

WHEN I WAS A CHILD I dreamt of a type of football that was dynamic and exciting. In my adult life, I have found my dream. English football represents all that football ought to be.

The game in England is steeped in history. There's a rivalry between the clubs that stretches back for generations. The football stadia are always full. The game is alive with passion and energy here.

Compared with what goes on elsewhere, English football is free from corruption. On the pitch, at any rate, there's an integrity which is seldom matched outside this country.

English football has its detractors. In recent years, critics have claimed that football in this country is not up to the level of its Continental and international counterparts. I dis-agree. I've always defended English football because I've always thought it was among the best in the world, both in the way it's organised and in the way some of the greater clubs here play the game.

English football

I'm pleased England did so well in the European Championship. It was a vindication of the beautiful, effective football that is played here. Contrary to what most people seem to believe, English football is the best technically, up there with the German game – and much better than in Italy, France or Spain. By technique I mean ball control, passing, crossing and the way goals are scored.

People bleat on about English football lacking imagination. I agree that compared to, say, the Brazilians or some other Latin-American teams, or a few of their European counterparts, the English lack a certain individual inventiveness. But they more than make up for it in the imaginative way that teams play as one. In places like France or Italy, you might find players with more individual flair; in the English game as it's played today, the emphasis is not on the genius of one or two brilliant individuals, but on developing the creative gifts of the team as a whole. English football is directed towards the front, it pushes the team forward; the aim is for the whole team to score a goal. This is the reverse of the tactic used on the Continent, where the aim is to put in place an ultra-defensive system in the hope that one or two players up front can make the difference.

Look at the way France played in the European Championship. They just waited for one of their star players to do something out of the ordinary and hung on grimly in the meantime. They played extremely defensively – negatively, even – and waited for the stroke of genius, the spark of imagination that would lift the match. It's not an easy system to play. And they didn't score a single goal in their last 240 minutes.

On the other hand, in England the idea is to get the whole team on the attack. That collective tactic ensures that there will be a lot of goals and a lot of action. It's pretty much end to end. The Italians, the French and the Spanish all rely on an individual player to make a difference, like a flash of lightning. It's much more effective to focus on the performance of the whole team than to base your strategy around the inspiration of an individual player. More effective and, in my opinion, more interesting for players and spectators alike. That's why I want to carry on playing English football. It represents all the qualities I strive for.

French football

FRENCH FOOTBALL IS TEETERING ON THE EDGE OF CATASTROPHE.
These days the French national side doesn't seem to have the sense of purpose and of aspiration which you see in the best teams. The problem is structural. It is striking that the twenty or so best French players don't play in France. [There has been an exodus of the top players to Italy and Spain in particular, for the 1996/97 season.] That sort of statistic is no accident, there has to be a reason for it. The people who run football in France are fully responsible for this exodus. These are the men who have the power to take decisions that matter, and these are the men that have so mismanaged French football that one can honestly say it's a complete failure.

This is only the beginning. Football is massively popular in France and it fuels the dreams of millions, especially among the young. For these fans, the National Championships are of crucial importance. They live for the beauty and the glory of the game. Young people in France relate to football – as the young do all over the world. It has become part of the social fabric. And this is a generation which is already growing up in France under the terrible spectre of proliferating drugs and increasing violence. Take away the national game, allow the fabric of football to fall apart and these problems can only get worse. What the administrators have to realise is that their responsibilities go well beyond the game itself. Football galvanises millions of young people, and it has come to mean something profound about life and living. Its mismanagement is intolerable.

The management of the national team is a reflection of the same problem. Selection is a mess. Theoretically, a national team should represent the best players a country has to offer. We all know that's not the way it works. It's up to the choice of an autocratic individual, or worse; at times he is just a puppet manipulated by factors that have little to do with football, such as finance or politics. Football can start to become a little like the Mafia. I myself have had my career affected by these manipulations, and frankly I find it fascinating to witness the workings of such a system at first hand.

The Players' Union

PLAYERS NEED REPRESENTATION. Diego Maradona and I got together to ensure that they got it. The international governing bodies never consult the players before making their decisions. We're not suggesting that we have to have a hand in every decision or that we have to run the show. But at the very least, our views have to be listened to. Football is not a dictatorship. But FIFA takes decisions as if they were the only ones who had a right to determine the game's destiny and that's not something we players should tolerate. Football should represent the most magnificent freedom for everybody. When important decisions are taken, there ought to be room for discussion.

Few players worry about this sort of involvement, but we felt that it was essential to take a stand. We're not doing it for ourselves, since I am well established and at the peak of my career at the age of thirty and Maradona is already thirty-five. We're doing it for the next generation of players, so they can have the opportunity to express themselves and to take their part in shaping the future of the beautiful game.

E. CANTONA

Diego Maradona

FOR ME, MARADONA REPRESENTS FOOTBALL. He is football. He is the greatest footballer of all time. People talk about Pelé, but for me there's no comparison. They say Pelé got three champions' medals in the World Cup, but the record books show that through injury or whatever his involvement was not always central in those squads. It's true that he was part of the team each time, and anyone who is part of a winning team deserves to share the glory. But in Maradona's case, he managed to win the World Cup without the sort of team and the calibre of team-mate that Pelé had at his disposal. In 1986, it was Maradona who carried Argentina to victory, and in 1990 he carried them to the final. In 1994, he was banned from playing in much of the competition. As soon as he left centre stage, most of the interest went out of the World Cup.

Rules

PEOPLE MAKE A SCANDAL out of the slightest incident. When Maradona scored that infamous goal with his hand in Mexico, the press had a field day. In England, Maradona has been condemned ever since for that act alone. From that day on, whatever he did was no good. Maradona's exceptional qualities go largely unreported in this country. In fact, that sort of incident is quite common: it's happened countless times, in England just as anywhere else. And if the English had got away with that themselves, we'd have heard no more about it. At least not in England.

If the truth be known, every footballer has tried to get away with something like that in their lives. None of us are proud of it, and no one said that Maradona was proud of it. But every day you see players getting away with murder. Ultimately it's the same as when you tackle someone from behind and the referee doesn't notice. Anyone who does that, or who tries to intimidate their opponent or the referee, goes beyond the laws of the game. Maradona did what he did and got away with it. Players get away with things all the time. English players are no exception.

Referees

Referees

REFEREES SOMETIMES GET IT RIGHT and sometimes they don't. It's as simple as that. I've made a lot of progress of late, as everyone knows. So I don't talk about this sort of thing so often any more. But there was a time when I used to lose my temper with referees. Not so much when they made honest mistakes: mistakes I can tolerate. After all, I make mistakes too; we're all human. But when I felt that there was an element of dishonesty my sense of fair play would be offended. The problems started when I felt that the mistake wasn't accidental, when I felt there was some sort of agenda at play.

Drugs & sport

THERE IS DEFINITELY A PROBLEM with drug-taking in sport. But there's also a problem with the procedures for testing people. We all know there are people who slip through the net for years on end. You hear stories about sportsmen who get caught only after four or five years of steroid abuse or who don't ever get caught – they have obviously eluded the testers. But on the other side of the coin, you only have to drink four or five cups of coffee to register as positive on some of these tests!

I fully accept that there has to be a check on substance abuse in sport, but the current arrangements don't work. The situation has got out of hand. If you're ill, you can't even take the appropriate remedy before a match. If you have a cold or a cough, there are medicines that could cure you, but they're banned and you just don't take them for fear of the tests. If someone catches a cold or needs a little help getting to sleep, they should be allowed to take the relevant medication without ruining their career.

People should make a distinction between different sorts of substance. If, say, someone takes sleeping tablets or smokes marijuana, that's their problem. Their performance won't be enhanced – quite the reverse. People don't take these substances to perform better, and banning them makes no sense to me. Against that, you have guys who take serious stuff, like anabolic steroids, and pass all the tests because they're also taking secondary products to disguise them.

Take Maradona. I think that when Maradona was banned from the World Cup it was a mistake on the part of the organising authorities. What he allegedly took was Ephedrine, a common cold remedy. If a person wanted to take performance-enhancing drugs, they'd hardly be likely to take a substance like that. Ephedrine is not exactly an evil substance. It is tolerated within some American sports. To be honest, I'm not even sure Maradona took the stuff. But assuming he did, surely if someone wanted to take drugs they'd take something that gave them an advantage on the field. You're hardly going to run the risk of being caught for a substance that has no effect on your performance.

Media & public opinion

Media & public opinion

THE MEDIA DO HAVE A ROLE TO PLAY. In football, for instance, it is essential that people should be well informed. It's the same in all aspects of life. But the power of the media can get out of hand.

Television stations, newspapers, big organisations and everyone else in a position of authority tries to manipulate public opinion. To some extent I have been caught up in this process. The media have tried to influence people against me more often than I care to mention. This is a phenomenon that goes way beyond football. After all, football's nothing compared to some of the things that are going on. It's not the be all and end all. When corruption is simply restricted to football, it's no big deal. When people start dying, that's when it gets serious. It happens distressingly often.

The media don't mention it because certain vested interests are always protected. And then years later, we discover that witnesses were assassinated, that people were condemned to death on trumped-up charges, all with the full protection of the media. Thirty years later, the truth comes out, when there's no longer any risk attached to speaking out, when there's no one left to prevent the story from surfacing. It's been repeated time and time again. We're getting used to it. And people have got the message that that's how it is; everyone's getting better and better at understanding how the system works.

We're getting to the stage where the more you try to manipulate, the less possible it becomes. Everyone knows that the power of the media can start to make people think anything. It can make people think that black is white. But the tactic has become so common that we're all becoming conscious of it, aware that it's existed for centuries. We seem to have got to a point today where people aren't taken in any more because they just don't want to be had. We're at a turning point, as people are gaining more and more understanding of the processes by which the powers-that-be seek to manipulate them. We're increasingly aware of who has the power and of the workings of that power. Bit by bit, people are learning to read between the lines, to pick up things in the spaces between the words and they're not letting themselves be deceived any more, at least not the majority.

In my own way, especially in France, I bear witness to all of this. I wouldn't say I was a victim of this process, but I've lived it and it's a fascinating position to be in. The more the media try to manipulate opinion against me, the more people like me. When journalists attack me they show their true colours. They reveal their hand, and people are shocked. I'm a living witness to the fact that people are beginning to understand how power works.

The trick, now, is to get people to speak out when it really makes a difference. Some years ago, I spoke out against Tapie (the former French Government minister and President of Olympique Marseille) when his power was at its highest point in France, and everyone said I was mad. You have no idea how difficult it was for me to speak out against him at that time, but it was important to rise to the challenge – I did it for football. It wasn't personal: the game was coming under threat and it had to be done so that young kids could continue to have their dreams. Today, Tapie is a spent force, he's almost a nobody now. He's being sued left, right and centre, and now all those people who were too terrified to raise their voices against him when it really mattered are joining the chorus of braying dogs. It's easy for them to do it now because there's no risk. But as far as I'm concerned, it's precisely because there's no risk that I don't mention him any more. What's the point in kicking people when they're down?

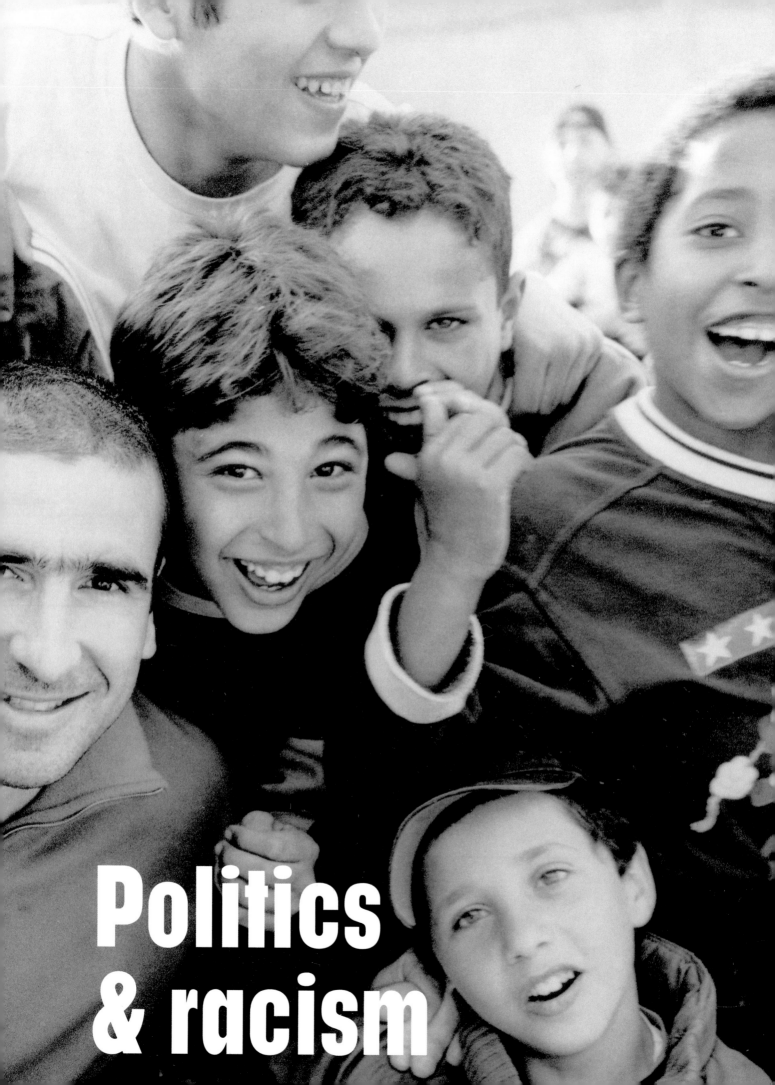

Politics
& racism

Politics & racism

CONVENTIONAL POLITICS MAY LEAVE ME COLD, but as a sporting personality, there is still a lot that one can do. For instance, I am very proud of participating in advertising campaigns that have a strong social message. The campaign I did for Nike against racism is one I feel especially pleased with.

Racism is something I can't come to terms with. I don't understand why people are afraid of different races coming together. When races come together, cultures are enriched. The richer the dialogue between cultures, the more we will all come to understand the world around us. Cultural diversity makes us smarter.

We need only look at contemporary music. Music's black roots and white roots are coming together to create new sounds and new rhythms, and the result is one of the most productive and dynamic periods in musical history. If white people had remained compartmentalised and refused to listen to black music, or if black people hadn't listened to white music, this would not have been possible.

Innovation is born out of dialogue and diversity. I don't know why people are so afraid of it. Racism is an abomination. And that's why I took the stand that I did, and agreed to do that advert — to let people know what the message is and to say that it isn't important what colour a person is. That's the sort of politics I feel I can engage with.

Advertising & sponsorship

Advertising & sponsorship

SPONSORSHIP IS BECOMING an increasingly important aspect of sport. I have nothing against that, but it does become a little strange when, as in the Atlanta Olympics, it's almost as if the battle of the sponsors was more important than the competition itself. However, the relationship between sport and sponsorship can be fruitful.

I get a lot of requests to promote products, but I take on only what I consider to be new; things I feel are going to be innovative or exciting, and things I'm going to enjoy. I don't just do advertisements because I want to make money, like some sportsmen. I don't need to.

People ask me if I cultivate an image. I say: "No. Image cultivates me." I'm not one of those personalities who get stuck with a particular image. Life always throws up something new, and the image I have at any given time is always part of a process of rethinking who I am. For some people, an image can be like a label. It can be a way for people to pigeon-hole you. I don't think I'm like that, and I don't think people can pigeon-hole me in quite that way. The moment they think

'66 WAS A GREAT YEAR FOR ENGLISH FOOTBALL. ERIC WAS BORN.

they know where I'm coming from, I change tack. I hate being stuck in a rut.

I'm proud of the work I've done for Nike, for instance, because it's always been bold, innovative material. Nike takes risks, it engages with issues. The adverts I have done reflect that. And the product mirrors that innovation: young people all over the world wear Nike. Nike represents the present and the future. Other companies are the past. They would never take such risks. They are afraid; they are obsessed with security. They play it safe. Everything Nike's advertisements do today, the competition will do in three years time. Everything they do today, Nike did three years ago. The designs reflect the same trends.

You have to take risks in life. That's what young people are all about. That's why young people wear Nike. They can't identify with a staid mentality. I am proud to be part of that movement of change, of

Money

MY ATTITUDE TOWARDS MONEY IS AMBIVALENT. I earn a lot of money playing football. Everyone knows that. When you have a lot of money like I do, you realise that it's necessary if you want to live a life that suits you, if you want to survive in a way that's right for you. After all, in a consumer society, money's important. We have to live with other people and, in society as we know it, that means we need money. Ironically, when you do have a lot of money, you realise that true value lies elsewhere. In the final analysis, money's worth nothing. You realise it's not what's really important. There's more to life. There are things money can't buy − like love and nature.

Money confuses things. It always creates problems between people and that's why it's hard to talk about. I'm taking a risk talking like this. It's easy to play down the value of wealth if you're rich. I know I'm speaking from a privileged position and some people might be offended by what I have to say. But as far as I'm concerned it's something that needs to be said.

Football has become a business like any other. It's part of the consumer society. The players take centre stage, so of course we have to get our share. Without us there would be no business. However, for the player, football will always be about something else. I earn a lot of money from playing football and so do many others. But if for some reason football wasn't part of the consumer society, if it had never become commercialised, we'd still play the game. We'd still cry when we lost. We'd still burst with joy whenever we won. We'd always be footballers because it's the game that we love. It's our life.

The early years

WHEN I JOINED AUXERRE, it was a young club; it had just been promoted to the French top division. I was attracted to the club because it seemed to be a place where a lot of attention was paid to young players. In a lot of French clubs at the time, especially the bigger clubs, the policy was to recruit the best players on offer and never to give younger players a chance to play in the first team. Auxerre was different. They had a commitment to youth and they seemed prepared to give youngsters a chance on the professional stage if they deserved it. So I went to Auxerre because I wanted to play first division football. I had the impression it was a place where young players were nurtured and were put in important positions so they could develop into top players.

It was there that I came into contact with the legendary Guy Roux. (He has been the club's manager for more than 30 years, during which time he has guided Auxerre from part-time regional football to win the Double of League Championship and Cup. Auxerre will represent France in the 1996/97 Champions' League). Auxerre was dominated by his benign presence. It wasn't so much because of the influence he had on me or other players, it was the fact that everyone had profound respect for him. He managed to build up a family atmosphere and everyone felt at home. I was about 400 miles from my home town, but he was like a father to me. He had the rare gift of being able to listen to young players. He never turned around and made you feel worthless, the way some elder statesmen in the game can. On the contrary, there was always a sense that he would take you under his wing. Sadly there are few people like that, especially nowadays. Roux was part of a dying breed. Today, society has become about getting a quick fix and moving on. It's common in many clubs to find a heartless attitude towards young players; an attitude in which they are used and then unceremoniously cast aside. Roux was different. His philosophy was to look after the young players, and I think that's essential in a football club.

After Auxerre, I had two spells at Marseille. The first was when I was twenty-two years old and just recently married. What happened there was a disaster, and I lay the blame for it firmly at my own door. I'd spent

The early years

eight years at Auxerre, and when I moved to Marseille it was the biggest transfer in French footballing history. Frankly, I couldn't deal with it.

My time there lasted six months — I knew I wasn't coping. It didn't work out because I thought I was some kind of big-shot. I worked just as hard as I ever do in training, but it was what I did between training sessions that was the problem. I'd spend my time doing other things, taking on this and that. I'd go off to night-clubs and, though I've never drunk excessively, I was beginning to burn the candle at both ends and to spread myself too thin. The city itself was having an effect on me. I was back in my home town, among childhood friends and family. There were always people around me. I like being with people but I can't stand being suffocated. My big mistake was to think I was bigger than football. I thought I was so talented that even if I spread myself thinly, I'd always find my feet. Except it can't be done. If you want to be the best, you have to concentrate on the task at hand. Being in Marseille started to be unbearable.

Once I realised that, I knew it was time for me to move on. I went to Montpellier. That season, we won the French Cup and it worked out very well. So when I went back to Marseille some months later, it was with a very different set of objectives. A year and a half had gone by in which I'd worked hard and I'd done a lot of necessary soul-searching. When I returned, I cut myself off from everything and focused on my playing.

It worked a treat until the end of that October. Then I sustained an injury, had to have an operation, and realised it was going to take me four or five months to get fit again. It was at that point that I came to realise that there were people around me, people I had grown to trust and respect, who made me feel that while I was injured, I no longer counted. Being injured wasn't the problem; it was the attitude of people around me that made me feel so angry. Once again, I felt I had to leave. The experience left me with a bitter after-taste. I don't like people who can treat others so callously. I didn't need them then, I don't need them now and I hope I never will need that sort of person. If ever I did have need of them, I'd rather die than accept help from them. I left and went on to play for Nîmes. And then... the rest, as they say, is history.

Family

WHEN I'VE HAD PROBLEMS to deal with, I've always had extraordinary support from my family. The family is one of the fundamental corner-stones of my life. The family represents stability, support, love. In times of trouble, I draw great strength from them. It's important to know that you're not on your own when times are hard. Love makes a family strong. If families stick together, they can share that strength and love.

Family

I come from a close-knit family. I continue to have strong ties with my parents and my brothers. There has never been the slightest trace of sibling rivalry between us. In some families, especially when one brother is more famous than another, there can be a petty-minded spirit of competition. That's never been the case between us. On the contrary, we've always tried to help one another. That's why when I hear about families in which there are rivalries or jealousies, I can understand it intellectually, but it makes me sad and I find it hard to reconcile it with my own experience.

I am grateful to my parents for a great deal. My childhood was exceptional because I never wanted for anything – we were never rich, but we had all the love we needed. We always had great respect for our parents without them ever having to raise a hand to us. Just a look was enough.

My parents were at pains to instil in me a sense of what was truly valuable. It is a lesson that has always stayed with me. They imbued us with a love of nature, of the simple things in life. In the end that's what we all come back to. As you get older, you come back to the most ancient traditions, to your relationship with the Earth and nature. Everything else is just superficial and we get attached to other things in a very shallow way. Nature costs nothing. If you love nature, if you feel an energy passing between you and nature, you can find it everywhere. It's something money can't buy.

I want to be able to pass on the same values to my children. I want to give them the sort of love my parents gave to me. I want them to learn the same respect for the family that I learned as a child. Of course, I also want them to be free. Freedom is the greatest gift you can bestow on a child. But there have to be certain limits: I want them to respect certain values in life. Once I can rest assured that they have learned to love those close to them, to respect others and to respect themselves; once I know that they can gain the respect of others and the love they deserve, they can do what they like. I will gladly let them be whatever they want. I want their imaginations to open up to the whole world. I want them to be free as long as their freedom doesn't impinge on the liberty of others.

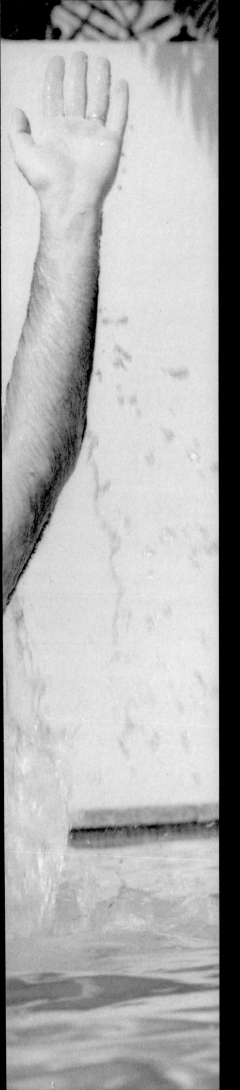

Anarchy

ABOVE ALL, I NEED TO BE FREE. I don't like to feel constrained by rules or conventions. Everyone has to live according to their own principles, but there's a limit to how far this idea can go. There's a fine line between freedom and chaos. To some extent I espouse the idea of anarchy. But it's never quite anarchy, there's always a little bit of order there. What I'm really after is an anarchy of thought, a liberation of the mind from all convention. Perhaps it ends up being more like surrealism than anarchy. It's like the way children think.

It would be wonderful if that sort of freedom were not limited to our innermost thoughts; if we could communicate with one another in that way too: the way children communicate. Picasso used to say: "It took me twenty years to learn to be a man, and sixty years to learn to be a child." When you're young all you want to do is grow up, but the older you get the more you realise you'd like to be a child again. Picasso was no anarchist, but he had something there; he understood the beauty of the spontaneity of childhood.

There's something magical about children. When children aren't manipulated by their parents, they speak the truth. I hate the way that some children can just become the product of their parents' ideas. When children are free, there's an incredible honesty about them. An honesty you can feel every time you come into contact with them. Honesty sets you free, and we should recover the freedom of childhood.

Friendship

THE FRIENDS I MADE AS A CHILD, before I became successful, are still my most important companions. When I was growing up, there were a lot of other kids in the same area and we would get together and play football. I have stayed in touch with many of them.

Since I've become famous, I've met many people I like a great deal. But when you're famous it's hard to know exactly who your friends are. I'm wary of other people; I know they might want something from me. There are people, both men and women, who are very good at pretending, and brilliant at taking you in, and who can make you believe that they are your friends. I don't trust them. That sort of friendship isn't genuine. That's why the friends that I have now are all people I knew before my career took off. With those people I know they like me for what I am, not for what I can do for them.

It happens of course that I meet people now and like them a lot. But I'm not prepared to be taken in by people and I don't want to wake up one morning and find out that I'm mistaken about someone and get a nasty shock. It doesn't mean I shut myself off completely, but a person in my position has to be careful. I have to protect myself.

There's a lot of talk about loyalty and faithfulness in friendship. I don't like that kind of talk. As far as I'm concerned, the loyalty we owe is to ourselves. What's important is being true to who we are and faithful to our beliefs.

On the pitch, what I believe in is winning. In order to win, you can't love your opponent. Even if I'm facing a friend on an opposing team, it doesn't matter to me. What I do before a match is to 'abstract' my opponent − neither to love him nor to hate him, but to focus on defeating him because that is what I have to do. It's about remembering that you play to win and it doesn't matter who's in your way. I am true to myself first and foremost.

Women

AS FAR AS I'M CONCERNED, women are a lot more intelligent than men. They're more intuitive. That's why women are striding ahead. The more women take positions of power – in politics, in the media, in public life in general – the more one can see how well suited they are to roles that only a short time ago were not available to them. Women deserve their success. We've always been taught that men are supposed to be macho, that they're supposed to be more powerful; but as time goes on, we're realising that women are a lot more competent than men.

The inner life

THERE IS AN INNER LIFE, the life of the spirit within. It's about discovering your true self, or rather somehow finding yourself again: often all that has happened is that you've lost sight of who you are. One's inner life is a way of learning to come to terms with oneself. It's only once you've learned to like yourself that you can start to like other people.

Utopia

I'M NOT AGAINST PROGRESS. You can't stop progress, but when it means that machines start to replace people in the workplace we have to be on our guard. The trick is to ensure that progress is working for us, working for people. What's the point of progress if all it leads to is misery for millions? The state has to take under its wing the people excluded by progress.

Unemployment is a terrible curse. So many things become difficult if you haven't got money: families start to argue, children lose their temper with their parents, parents lose their temper with their children; the kids end up hanging around in streets and are surrounded by others who have no money. There are tensions which lead to violence and to crime. In the perfect society even people who don't work would have enough money to be happy.

I accept that it would be difficult for everyone to earn a lot of money. But in my Utopia, at the very least those who cannot work would have a minimum standard of living: at the very least, enough to eat well and to have the right kind of living environment. It's when we fail to guarantee that much that we end up with the appalling social problems that we face today.

In a perfect society, people would be given the means to express themselves creatively. There would be centres where people could learn about music and the arts. Treat people decently and there would be a lot less violence and drug abuse. People would open their minds. Just because people don't work, that doesn't mean that you can't make their lives better. If you do, you make everyone's life better. That's Utopia.

Success

IF I PERFORM VERY WELL in a football match but my side loses, I can't possibly be happy. Some players seem to feel it's fine to be pleased with a strong individual performance. As far as I'm concerned, if the team wins, then and only then do I allow myself the luxury of feeling pleased with myself for certain small details that may have led to that success. But winning is something that's ultimately more important than my own happiness.

Self-belief

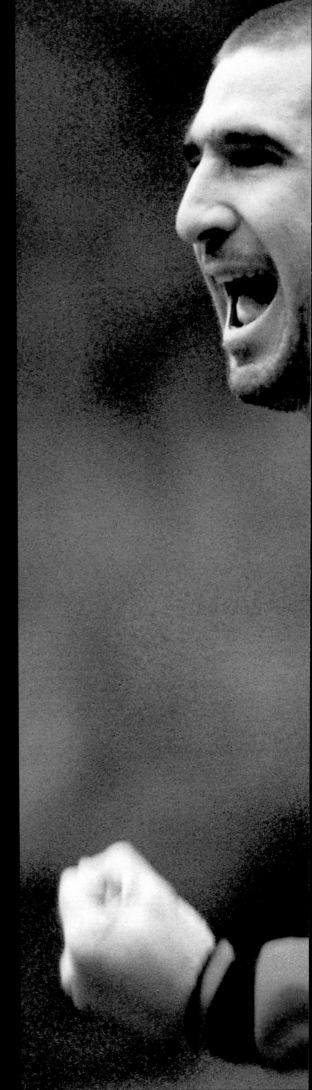

I'VE SAID IN THE PAST that I could play single-handedly against eleven players and win. I believe in myself. Sometimes it's crazy, I know. Give me a bicycle and I believe that I can beat Chris Boardman's one-hour record. If someone says to me, "Get on this bicycle and beat the world record," I say: "OK. I've got a chance." It is that belief which drives me on. No matter what the situation, I always think I have a chance of winning.

Victory is all-important, and to succeed you have to believe.

There is a place for doubt: doubt makes you question yourself, it makes you want to win. Doubt leads to fear, and fear is what fuels every great challenge. But the trick is to transcend that fear, to believe in your own abilities so that the team can win. I've always had that quality. Even if it's crazy, it's part of who I am. There's something inside me that always believes I can do it.

Cinema

THE CINEMA IS ANOTHER OF MY ENDURING PASSIONS. Some day, I'd love to make films myself − I'd like to have the talent to direct. I know it's not something everyone has, and I'm not sure I have it. But I'd love to try it out. One day I know I'll have a go. I'll get together with friends and write my own screenplay for a short film, just to see what turns out. I'll produce the film myself so that nothing gets imposed on me and t`ry to bring to life some of the ideas about film-making I have in my head. The hope is that I would be able to do it the way I can see it in my mind. That's the hard bit − it seldom happens, but I'd like to get as close as possible to that ideal.

In current cinema, Mickey Rourke is someone I like very much − both as an actor and as a person. I am impressed by the way he remains true to himself, even when his opposition to the establishment or to established ways of doing things makes his role quite difficult. I like actors and actresses who give off a certain passionate sense of who they are and who remain true to themselves whatever the part they portray. That passion is what I like best about the cinema.

After football

WHEN I STOP PLAYING FOOTBALL I don't want to have to work ever again. I'll put money in the bank, let it generate interest and live on that for the rest of my life. No one will tell me what to do. I won't have a boss and I'll be able to do whatever I like.

When I do quit football it'll be at the very top. I never want to slip below the top in my professional career. I certainly wouldn't contemplate playing for teams that are any less successful than Manchester United. Nor would I contemplate playing for the reserves. Once I feel I'm not at the top any more, I'll quit football.

I haven't yet decided if I would contemplate becoming a football manager. If I did, it would be on the strict condition that I could bring something new to the game. I would never contemplate becoming a manager simply to do what other managers have done before me. All my life I've wanted to do new things, to break new ground. If ever I had the sense that I could do this as a manager, I'd certainly consider it.

Many former players have become successful managers. Players like Beckenbauer and Cruyff have brought something new to football. They've added something because they've known how to make football progress and how to ensure the progress of those who play under them. There is a special talent involved in saying something to a player that no one has ever said before. Getting help from others is a good thing, but it's even better to know how to give help oneself. If when I retire from football I have the sense that I really have something to give to the game and to its next generation of young players, then becoming a manager is certainly something I wouldn't rule out.

Beyond football

I DO A NUMBER OF THINGS BESIDES FOOTBALL, it's true, but I'm careful about how I handle all my different interests. There have been times in my life when I have spread myself very thin and lost sight of what I'm really good at... which is football. Now that I am older and I have a bit of experience under my belt, I've learned how to maintain the right balance. I operate under the principle that I can do anything I enjoy, so long as it doesn't interfere with my game. Whatever I do cannot become more important than football, and certainly must not diminish my possibilities in the game. Of all

As for other things, I enjoy trying things out. I do a bit of painting, for instance, and I like to draw. That much is well known about me. But under no circumstances would I ever refer to myself as a painter or an artist. I have too much respect for great artists to count myself among them. I dabble for pleasure. It's the same with poetry. Poets are important people. They achieve extraordinary things with words. They're far too important for me to go around calling myself a poet. I'm just an amateur when it comes to poetry. It would be like someone who enjoys the odd game of football on a Sunday afternoon, or who messes about in the street playing football with his friends, calling himself a footballer. Even if he's a good-ish player, it's not appropriate. There's such a thing as an amateur footballer and such a thing as a professional. I am a professional. When it comes to football, nothing else can stand in the way of that.

In my spare time, though, there's a lot that I enjoy. Music for instance. I like a wide range of music. It depends on how I am feeling. Sometimes I like calm music, classical music; sometimes I like pop music, sometimes opera. I often listen to the car radio and I enjoy listening to whatever's on offer. But at home, I choose my music carefully to match the mood I'm in. I listen to a lot of British and American bands. But every so often, I feel the need to listen to French lyrics, to hear words sung in my native language.

Art is another thing I derive great pleasure from. I like Picasso, Mirò, Kandinsky. I like all the painters of the Cobra generation, that last great generation of modernist painters – people like Karel Appel, Corneille and Lindstrom.

It was my father who instilled a great love of painting in me. He too is a painter. But to an extent I've developed my taste in art as a reaction to the images I was familiar with as a small child. When I was younger, we had dozens of books in the house about art. Many of them were about Impressionism, which was the vogue among my father's generation. I was very little at the time I became aware of these books and I think I was too young when I got to know these painters. In a sense I've evolved away from them. That is, I don't know if it's really an evolution; but a certain moment in my life, I felt I had to move on. I felt I needed something else, another style to express my individuality.

Growing old

I'M NOT AFRAID of growing old. I think I'd be able to adapt to old age, just as I've been able to adapt to all the stages of my life so far. But if there is something that frightens me, it's the idea that one day I'll die, that some day I'll simply disappear. It's not so much that I'm afraid of death itself, it's more that I love life too much. And what frightens me isn't dying so much as not living any more. It's not death itself, not the darkness of death that worries me, but the thought of no longer existing in the bright light of living.

If, as some people think, there is such a thing as reincarnation, I'd love to come back. It would fascinate me to live in someone else's body, not necessarily someone famous. In fact, it needn't even be a human being. Given a choice, I'd come back as an eagle. I love the way eagles move; the way they soar, the way they gaze.

Photography